love letters

a thousand reasons why I love you

EMMA ROSE

Copyright © 2024 by Chapter Zero

All rights reserved – No portion of this book may be reproduced in any form without written permission from the publisher or author, except as permitted by U.S. copyright law.

Published by Chapter Zero LLC
16192 Coastal Highway, Lewes, Delaware – USA
info@chapterzerobooks.com

Paperback ISBN 978-1-961963-21-4
Hardcover ISBN 978-1-961963-22-1

Love is when you care,
When the world fades away,
And it's just the two of you.

Holding hands, sharing dreams,
Every word a song you sing together,
Every smile a reason to keep going.

Love is trust, unspoken yet clear,
Seeing faith in each other's eyes,
Feeling safe in each other's touch.

It's not about grand gestures,
But the little moments,
When their absence feels like a void,
And their presence, a warm embrace.

A simple text, a loving glance,
Bringing back joy,
Covering the miles of life's journey,
With love as your constant guide.

Introduction

Sometimes, we find ourselves at a loss for words, struggling to express the depth of our love. In those moments, it's not because our feelings are absent, but because they are so profound, they defy language. This book is for those times. "Love Letters" offers the words you seek to celebrate the extraordinary bond you share with your partner.

Through heartfelt expressions, this collection captures the essence of love in its many forms. From the joy of shared adventures to the comfort of quiet moments, these pages hold the sentiments we often find difficult to articulate. Let this book be your voice, conveying your love in ways that resonate deeply and honestly. Whether it's for a special occasion or a simple reminder of your affection, these love letters are here to help you say, "I love you," in the most meaningful way.

My life began
the moment I met you.
Colors seemed brighter,
the world felt new.

In your eyes, I found my home,
in your touch, I discovered warmth,
in your smile, I saw my future.

Every day since then,
has been a journey of us,
together, writing our love story.

EMMA ROSE

My soulmate,
you've given my life
a new meaning.
Each day, I cherish you more,
and I know our love
is meant to last
forever.

LOVE LETTERS

My love,
I adore our future talks.
Your enthusiasm
lights up my life.
Every day is brighter,
because you are *my sunshine*.

EMMA ROSE

You
are the first thing
I think about,
each morning
and every night.
You are a *part of me*,
and forever will be.

LOVE LETTERS

When you hold my hand,
I feel so safe and protected.
You're *my rock*
when things get tough,
my calm in the chaos.

EMMA ROSE

The way
you listen to me,
makes me feel
truly valued.
You hear my every word,
and I've never felt
more understood.

LOVE LETTERS

Thank you
for knowing when
I need a hug,
for holding me
when I'm overwhelmed.
Your kindness
never goes unnoticed,
it means the world to me.

EMMA ROSE

I love our quiet mornings
and late-night talks.
Those simple moments
mean everything to me.
It's when our love
feels the strongest,
turning the ordinary
into *something magical*.

LOVE LETTERS

You inspire me
to be *my best self*.
Your belief in me
gives me confidence,
and I never knew
I could be this strong
until you showed me.

EMMA ROSE

Your hugs
are my *safe haven*,
where I find peace and love.
In your arms,
I'm home,
and I never want to leave.

LOVE LETTERS

Every passing minute
brings you *closer to me*.

From being strangers to sharing our joy,
you've left a deep impression on my soul.

The more I know about you,
the more I keep falling in love with you.

EMMA ROSE

I can't wait
to spend every Christmas
with you,
placing gifts under the tree,
and *watching your smile*
light up the room.

My love,
thank you for always
supporting my dreams,
and encouraging me
to chase what I love.
Your belief in me
gives me the strength
to keep dreaming
and pursuing my goals.

EMMA ROSE

Every kiss with you
feels like our first.
Our hearts were melting,
time stood still,
and the clocks stopped.
It's still the same with you,
and it forever will be.

LOVE LETTERS

What did I think about
before you came along?
Now, *every thought is you.*

You've filled my mind,
my heart, my world,
and I can't imagine it any other way.

EMMA ROSE

Tell the world we got it right,
I choose you,
you are mine and I am yours,
I choose you.

We aren't perfect,
but we'll learn together.
No matter how long it takes,
I'll prove my love to you.

LOVE LETTERS

I'd choose you in every lifetime,
in every world, in every dream.
No matter where, no matter when,
it's you I'd always choose again.

EMMA ROSE

There's nothing I want more
than to make you the happiest person
in the world.

Your smile is my goal,
your joy, my mission.
I just want to see you happy,
every single day.

LOVE LETTERS

You are *one of a kind*,
there's no category for you.
Unique in every way,
you stand out like no one else.

In a world full of copies,
you are the original,
and I'm so grateful
to have you in my life.

EMMA ROSE

Honey,
thank you for cooking for me.
Your meals have a special flavor,
and I can tell
they're *made with love.*
I taste your love in every bite,
and it's a gift I cherish deeply.

Your strength
during tough times
makes me want
to be braver.
You're the one
I look up to,
you are my inspiration.

EMMA ROSE

Holding *your hand in mine*
makes me feel safe and loved.
No matter where we are,
your touch grounds me
and makes everything
feel right.

LOVE LETTERS

My one and only,
I love you because,
You bring out *the best in me*,
always helping me to grow.
You make me a better person,
every single day.

EMMA ROSE

Planning our future together
fills me with excitement and hope.
Every dream we share
brings us closer,
and makes me love you
even more.

LOVE LETTERS

The way *you make me laugh*,
even when I don't feel like smiling,
Is one of the many reasons,
I love you so much.

EMMA ROSE

I'm in love with you
and the person you are.
It doesn't matter how you look,
or who you want to be.
What matters is *your heart*,
and I know it's true.

I've never met
someone as genuine as you,
and that's why
I'm drawn to you.
I love your simplicity,
and the way you live your life.

LOVE LETTERS

I just love exploring
new places with you,
because your sense of adventure
makes every single trip
unforgettable.

EMMA ROSE

The way you look at me,
with so much *love and tenderness,*
makes me feel
like the luckiest person
in the world.

LOVE LETTERS

During our late-night talks,
your voice
soothes my soul
like moonlight in the dark,
making everything
feel right.

EMMA ROSE

My love,
I would do anything
to *see you smile*.
Your smile
is my favorite thing
in the whole world.

LOVE LETTERS

Every moment with you
has been amazing,
but I promise you this,

the best is yet to come.

Our journey has just begun,
and the future holds
even more incredible times.

EMMA ROSE

Your hugs
after a long day,
melt all my stress away.
You're my peace.

LOVE LETTERS

In my darkest moments,
It's your voice that brings me calm,
Your presence that gives me ,
Your love that lights the way.

With you by my side,
no challenge feels too great,
no fear too overwhelming.
Together, we can face anything.

EMMA ROSE

The *connection* we have
is so rare in this world.
We don't need words
to communicate;
our eyes speak volumes
to each other.

LOVE LETTERS

Whenever we go to see a movie,
and I hold your hand
in that dark room,
all I can think about is *us*.
I just want to kiss you
and forget about the film.

EMMA ROSE

You're *a real blessing* for my mind.
To be honest,
I couldn't have faced my battles
without you by my side.
I'm deeply grateful for your presence,
and I hope I'll always be worthy
of being with such a beautiful soul,
in my life.
That's all I could ever ask for.

LOVE LETTERS

My love,
I wake up
looking forward to *your message*.
Your words
brighten my day,
and I'm so thankful
to have you in my life.

EMMA ROSE

Meeting you changed everything,
I see life through a new lens.
Your love paints my world,
bringing light to every shadow.

LOVE LETTERS

You are
the most amazing person
I have ever known,
and I can't believe
that I'm the one who got you.

I can't think of any better way
to spend my life
than with you at my side.

EMMA ROSE

Goodnight messages from you
mean everything to me.
Knowing you think of me
warms my heart deeply.

LOVE LETTERS

Love can't change you,
but it changes something in you.
Like you did for me,
I wasn't like this before,
But now,
you've become *a part of me.*

EMMA ROSE

It's so sweet
when you send me songs
during the day.
Knowing that certain songs
make you *think of us*
fills me with so much
hope for our future together.

LOVE LETTERS

I thought I knew love before,
but only after I met you
did I truly understand.

Your presence revealed new depths,
emotions I never knew existed,
a *warmth that fills my soul*.

Every glance, every touch,
taught me what love really means,
a bond so deep,
it changed everything.

EMMA ROSE

Our morning coffee chats
are simple,
yet so precious.
I cherish every sip with you
because it's *your presence*
that makes everything so special.

LOVE LETTERS

That first night, something stirred,
a feeling so rare, so new.
In that moment, I knew,
our story was just beginning.

EMMA ROSE

I love
how you *listen to me*,
truly hearing my thoughts.
You make me feel
valued and understood,
like no one else.

LOVE LETTERS

Our late-night drives,
talking about life and dreams,
are everything to me.
Those moments are gold,
with the world quiet around us,
and *just us*
in our own little bubble.

EMMA ROSE

Walking in the city with you,
hand in hand,
your eyes light up the world
around us,
like two bright stars
guiding our way.

LOVE LETTERS

Life together isn't always easy,
but with you, *it's always worth it*.
Through and sunny days,
your hand in mine makes it all okay.

Challenges come and go,
but your love remains my anchor,
In your arms, I find strength,
and in your heart, I find my home.

EMMA ROSE

Seeing your name
on my screen,
always makes me happy.
You are *my favorite notification*.

LOVE LETTERS

Cuddling on the couch,
watching our favorite shows
after a long day,
is what I need
to feel better.

EMMA ROSE

Sometimes I ask myself
why I fell in love with you
in the first place
and the only thing comes to my mind
is *your beautiful eyes*,
the day I met you.

LOVE LETTERS

Your special scent
makes me wanna
kiss your neck
for hours.

EMMA ROSE

Holding hands in public,
and showing you my affection,
shows the world you're mine
and *I'm yours*.
We belong together.

I cannot imagine life,
with someone else,
but *you*.
Honestly,
it's always been you,
and forever, will be.

EMMA ROSE

In your light,
each day finds purpose,
and, *without you*,
my life feels like
an endless darkness.

LOVE LETTERS

Your lips,
they're like my cherry orchard,
Always so sweet,
always so ripe,
Every kiss feels like
the juiciest fruit,
all year round.

EMMA ROSE

Every time
you *say my name*,
it sounds like a love song.

LOVE LETTERS

You know,
it might sound cheesy,
but, I can't picture my life
without you in it.
You're like *the missing puzzle piece*,
The one that completes the picture
of my world.

EMMA ROSE

Those little moments,
when you hold my hand,
while you are driving,
are everything I dream about,
all day long.

LOVE LETTERS

Your gentle touch,
Calms my anxious heart.
In your closeness,
I find my peace, my start.

EMMA ROSE

Your beautiful voice
on the phone,
is my favorite sound
I could listen to,
forever.

LOVE LETTERS

When I'm with you,
the chaos fades away,
and peace washes over me.
Like the *calm before a storm*,
but in the best possible way.

EMMA ROSE

You made my dreams a reality,
The moment you said those three words,
"I love you," became my anthem,
And every day feels like a dream,
That I never want to wake up from.

LOVE LETTERS

Every morning I wake up,
I'm in awe of the love we share.
It's like living in a movie,
but better, because it's real.
Because it's with *you*.

EMMA ROSE

When I gaze into your eyes,
I see a future filled
with *endless possibilities*,
A world where we chase our dreams,
and create memories that last a lifetime.
It's a vision I never want to let go of,
because with you,
anything is possible.

LOVE LETTERS

You are
my anchor
in a sea of uncertainty.

EMMA ROSE

I want to *travel the world*
with you,
make love in every city,
and leave our scent
in all hotel rooms.

LOVE LETTERS

Time stands still with you,
every moment feels right.
Just us, and nothing more,
you are all I need, my light.

EMMA ROSE

Thank you
for sending photos and updates
every day.
It makes me feel
like I'm *right there with you*,
even though we're miles apart.

With you, *I don't fear silence*,
it's a comfort, not a void.
In the quiet moments, side by side,
our hearts speak louder than words.

No need for constant chatter,
your presence is enough.
In the stillness, I find peace,
with you, silence feels like home.

EMMA ROSE

I love you for who you are,
your authenticity shines bright.
In a world full of masks,
you remain true to yourself.

LOVE LETTERS

You're my favorite adventure,
my partner in crime.
With you by my side,
life's always exciting.

EMMA ROSE

My love,
your morning messages
is what I wake up for.
Your words light up my world,
and I'm so grateful
to have you in my life.

LOVE LETTERS

Honestly, I'm amazed
by how much *you mean to me.*
Every day, I'm grateful,
for your love and presence.

EMMA ROSE

When I'm with you,
time stands still.
It's like the world fades away,
and it's just
you and me.

LOVE LETTERS

Only you know me so well,
that my unspoken words are clear.

You see *through my masks*,
understanding my fears and dreams.

You're always there when I need,
no need to ask, you just know.

EMMA ROSE

I love
the way you laugh,
the way you make me laugh,
and how you *brighten my world*.

LOVE LETTERS

You've turned
my dreams into reality.
just by loving me,
you've made
everything possible.

EMMA ROSE

I don't know
if you realize it,
but you bring
so much *joy to my life*.
I'm truly blessed
to have you
by my side.

Honestly,
you've swept me off my feet,
every day feels *like a dream*,
since you walked into my life.

EMMA ROSE

We rarely argue,
but when we do,
I love how we find our way back.

Through calm words and gentle touches,
we mend the rifts,
finding peace in our understanding.

It's in those moments,
I see the strength of our love,
and how *we always choose us*.

LOVE LETTERS

I once doubted love's existence,
but with you, my doubts fade.
You make me a believer,
in a bond that's beautifully made.

EMMA ROSE

I love
how we cuddle in the morning,
wrapped up *in each other's arms*,
and your voice, all raspy and soft,
whispering sweet words in my ear.

LOVE LETTERS

I love spending rainy days
at home with you,
With the smell of coffee filling the air,
it's those simple moments that I treasure.
Cuddled up on the couch,
watching the rain,
listening to its soothing rhythm on the roof.
Rainy days are my favorite,
when it's *with you*.

EMMA ROSE

Your *morning kisses*,
are like sunshine on my skin.
Waking up to your love,
is the best way to begin.

LOVE LETTERS

Lost in your eyes,
I find my reflection.
With you,
I see myself,
and it's a *beautiful connection*.

EMMA ROSE

I love you
for *all your perfect imperfections,*
For the way you snort when you laugh,
And how you sing off-key in the shower,
I love you
for your messy hair in the morning,
and the way you wear mismatched socks.
For the little things
that make you uniquely you,
I love you
for who you truly are.

LOVE LETTERS

When I'm in your arms,
everything feels right.
It's like the world fades away,
and all that matters
is us.

EMMA ROSE

Sitting under the stars
with you,
I feel like we're the only ones in the world.
It's *just you and me,*
and our love
lighting up the night sky.

LOVE LETTERS

Sending you a text,
is like sending you
a piece of my heart.
Even though we're apart,
I feel I'm there with you,
wherever you are.

EMMA ROSE

Saying goodnight to you,
is the hardest part of my day.
But knowing *I'll dream of you*,
makes it a little easier to bear.

LOVE LETTERS

When I kiss you,
it's like time stops.
Our lips meet,
and the world fades away.

EMMA ROSE

Sundays with you,
lazy and easy,
no plans, just us and our coffee.
Lounging around
in our comfy clothes,
no rush, no stress,
just pure relaxation.
With nowhere to go
and nothing to do,
just enjoying the simple pleasure
of *being together*.

LOVE LETTERS

Locking eyes with you,
I see love
reflected back at me.
It's an unspoken language,
that speaks volumes of our connection.

EMMA ROSE

Your scent on my skin,
your breath against mine,
It's like...
I can't even explain,
but it's like everything stops,
And all I can feel is *you*,
taking my breath away.

LOVE LETTERS

I wish I'd known you earlier,
I missed you before we even met.
In my heart, there was a space,
only you could fill, *my perfect fit*.

EMMA ROSE

When I look into your eyes,
my heart just stops,
It doesn't matter where we are.

Whether we're at a coffee shop,
waiting for our cheesecake and coffee,
or sitting in a restaurant,
waiting for our food to arrive.

Your eyes,
they're just mesmerizing,
And in that moment,
all I wanna do
is melt into your arms,
No matter where we are.

LOVE LETTERS

I'll always remember
our first kiss,
we were both so shy and uncertain,
afraid of what it might mean,

I feared losing you,
feared giving you my heart,
but I took the leap,
and look at us now,
together, for so long,
still standing strong,
and still deeply in love,
just like that *first kiss.*

EMMA ROSE

Even though we're miles apart,
I can't help but *dream of our future*,
of cooking your favorite meals,
and brewing your morning coffee just right,
of snuggling with you in bed,
until the sun peeks through the curtains,
and our love fills the room
with warmth.

LOVE LETTERS

It might seem weird,
but I love hitting the stores with you.
You're patient and always curious
about what catches my eye.
I can tell *you care about me*,
And honestly,
I wouldn't want to go shopping
with anyone else but you.

EMMA ROSE

I'm dreaming of us
making our first snowman,
with snowflakes
tickling your cute nose,
I'll warm your hands with mine,
then we'll sip tea in our cozy home,
by the crackling fireplace.

LOVE LETTERS

Sometimes,
I can't help but wonder,
what life would be like,
without you by my side,
and then I realize,
my eyes are already misty,
jst at the thought of it.
I love you.

EMMA ROSE

I wanna grow old with you,
and spend my whole life
by your side,
day and night,
never getting tired of us,
'cause life's just magical *with you*.

LOVE LETTERS

Every now and then,
I find myself asking,
what have I done
to deserve someone like you?

Then, I count my lucky stars,
grateful for the miracle,
that is *you, in my life*.

EMMA ROSE

When you get out early,
I love to *sleep on your pillow*,
it still holds your warmth,
and brings me close to you.

LOVE LETTERS

Sometimes I miss you like crazy,
and all I can do
is stare at your pictures,
I find myself lost in the memory of your lips,
but then I remember that soon,
we'll be together again,
and suddenly,
hope floods my heart once more.

EMMA ROSE

Thoughts of you
fill my heart with joy.
A day spent by your side
is all I ever need.
You are my happy place,
where everything feels right,
and nothing could be better.

I love it when you hold my hand,
especially when I'm nervous
about taking off
or landing in an airplane.

You know me inside out,
you know I'm not the best at it,
but I know that you're always there for me,
no matter what,
and it warms my heart.

EMMA ROSE

Our love isn't bound
by hours or days,
it's *a timeless connection*.
We'll find each other again,
in a place beyond time.

LOVE LETTERS

Thank you for every day
you've made me feel loved,
cherished, and appreciated.

Words fall short,
but my heart is full.
grateful to have you,
now and always.

EMMA ROSE

I live to *see you smile*,
your happiness is my goal,
because you're the reason,
my heart feels whole.

LOVE LETTERS

Everyone's got their reason
to get up in the morning,
to tackle the day.

You're my motivation,
the spark that gets me going.

Thinking of you starts my day,
and that's all I need,
to face the world with a smile.

EMMA ROSE

Our souls are *forever linked*.
Even when we're not together,
we'll always find our way back,
to a place where love never fades.

I can be surrounded by many,
but it's your voice,
that feels *like home*.

EMMA ROSE

Some people
can't understand our love,
but that doesn't matter to me.
What we share
is beyond words,
a connection so deep,
only we can feel.

They might not see
what we see,
But *our love is real*,
unshakeable,
a bond that grows stronger,
with every heartbeat,
every breath.

LOVE LETTERS

In a world
full of doubts,
your love stands,
unquestioned.

EMMA ROSE

I'll be the one
whispering "baby" in the dark,
Standing beside you,
ready to face any storm.

I'll be the one
your heart grows to cherish,
the thought that lingers in your mind.

Just let me know when,
tell me where,
and *I'll be there, always,*
ready to hold you close.

LOVE LETTERS

You're my first light,
my gentle dawn,
the reason I rise,
and face the day with hope.

EMMA ROSE

Our long video calls at night
are the sweetest
part of my day.
I love how we are trying
to make it work.

LOVE LETTERS

Your lips on mine,
soft and sweet,
sending shivers down my spine,
and making my heart skip a beat.
Like butterflies in my stomach,
fluttering and alive,
your kiss,
a gentle touch,
leaving me breathless,
and lost in time.

EMMA ROSE

Every thought of you,
brings a smile to my face.
You're *my sweetest addiction*.

LOVE LETTERS

From the start,
to this very moment,
my heart has always been yours.

Now and forever,
you are my every heartbeat,
my eternal love.

EMMA ROSE

I must confess that sometimes,
I get jealous of all the poeple
who get to see you
and talk to you
every single day.
But then I remember,
I have your heart,
and suddenly, everything's alright.

LOVE LETTERS

Making memories
with you,
is my favorite thing to do,
From sunrise to sunset,
every shared moment,
is a *treasure*
I'll never forget.

EMMA ROSE

At first,
I was scared to love again,
afraid to trust
after being hurt before,
but you've proven to me,
each and every day,
that it's all worth it.
And it always will be,
because *you're a rare soul*,
like no other.

LOVE LETTERS

I want to give you
everything I have,
My body and my soul,
because you've touched me
with a passion so genuine,
so pure,
that I trust you completely.
You're my *safe place*.

EMMA ROSE

A thousand conversations,
none compare,
to *your one sweet word*.

I ache for you all the time, babe.
Your absence
just leaves this big hole in me,
every day without you feels like forever.

I just wanna feel you near,
hold you close,
hear your voice in my ear.

I miss you so much it hurts,
and I can't wait till we're back together,
'cause you're like
the missing piece of me.

EMMA ROSE

I think
I'm the luckiest person in the universe,
because I have you by my side.
You're beautiful, inside and out,
and I love you for who you are.

LOVE LETTERS

I hope this never changes,
you, just as you are.

Every moment with you,
feels fresh, like morning dew.

I've told you before,
I'll tell you again,
it's you, and only you.

My love remains,
unchanged, unwavering,
until the end.

Thanks!

Dear reader,

Thank you for joining me on this journey of love and connection. I hope "Love Letters: A thousand reasons why I love you" has helped you express your deepest feelings and brought you closer to your partner.

If this book has touched your heart, I would be grateful if you could share your experience with a review on Amazon. Your feedback means the world to me and can help other couples discover the beauty of expressing their love. Writing a review is a simple yet meaningful way to support both me and fellow readers.

May your days be filled with love, joy, and unforgettable moments.

With heartfelt thanks,

Emma Rose

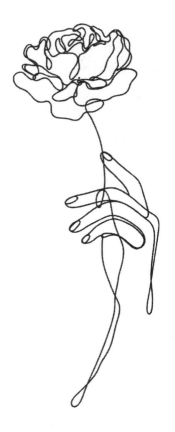

Made in the USA
Monee, IL
16 December 2024

19818be1-1de9-480f-a45f-7c3d8d5d5700R01